the PIPER

PIPER
the

The Epic Betrayal of Biblical Consequence

DENNIS BANK

NEW YORK

the PIPER
The Epic Betrayal of Biblical Consequence

Published in New York, New York, by Morgan James Publishing. Morgan James
and The Entrepreneurial Publisher are trademarks of Morgan James, LLC.
www.MorganJamesPublishing.com

The Morgan James Speakers Group can bring authors to your live event. For more
information or to book an event visit The Morgan James Speakers Group at
www.TheMorganJamesSpeakersGroup.com.

ISBN 978-1-61448-806-4 paperback
ISBN 978-1-61448-807-1 eBook
Library of Congress Control Number: 2013944421

Cover Design by:
Rachel Lopez
www.r2cdesign.com

Interior Design by:
Bonnie Bushman
bonnie@caboodlegraphics.com

FREE eBook edition for your
existing eReader with purchase

PRINT NAME ABOVE

For more information,
instructions, restrictions, and
to register your copy, go to
www.bitlit.ca/readers/register
or use your QR Reader to scan
the barcode:

In an effort to support local communities, raise awareness and funds, Morgan James
Publishing donates a percentage of all book sales for the life of each book to Habitat for
Humanity Peninsula and Greater Williamsburg.

Get involved today, visit
www.MorganJamesBuilds.com.

Habitat
for Humanity®
Peninsula and
Greater Williamsburg
Building Partner

CONTENTS

DECEPTION'S DOOR

S atan can't override the authority of the Word of God, but he is very good at twisting its interpretation to bolster his own kingdom. He first tried it with Adam and Eve, and he succeeded. This first deception in the Bible resulted in the first sin and the fall of man. Four thousand years later, Satan tried it again, this time with Jesus Christ, but he soon found out he was no match for the Messiah, who easily overcame him. How? Jesus, demonstrating the power of the written Word of God, simply quoted to the devil what was written in the Scriptures.

Then the devil taketh him up into the holy city, and setteth him on a pinnacle of the temple, And saith unto him, If thou be the Son of God, cast thyself down: for it is written, He shall give his angels charge concerning thee: and in their hands they shall bear thee up, lest at any time thou dash thy foot against a stone. **Jesus said unto him, It is written again, Thou shalt not tempt the Lord thy God**. Again, the devil taketh him up into an exceeding high mountain, and sheweth him all the kingdoms of the world, and the glory of them; And saith unto him, All these things will I give thee, if thou wilt fall down and worship me. **Then saith Jesus unto him, Get thee hence, Satan: for it is written, Thou shalt worship the Lord thy God, and him only shalt thou serve.**

Matthew 4:5-10, AKJV

Make no mistake, Satan is still up to the same old tactic, but the question is will we be observant enough to challenge him when he tries it with us? Or is there a chance that we have already been duped? Satan already misleads the world through various religions and factions, but what if he could do just one thing to throw all Christianity off course? What if he could reword the living Scriptures in such a manner that even the most intellectual of theologians wouldn't notice the life-altering changes? With the Bible being the size it is, how does one get past the wonderful wording of a new

Bible translation to discern if a well-organized special interest group hasn't changed the message as intended from the King of Kings?

In *The Piper* we will use side-by-side Scripture texts to show how the Authorized King James Version (AKJV) and the popular modern translations differ—something even the most devout believer might not notice until seeing them juxtaposed. Although there are many, we will zero in on twenty-four key doctrinal teachings, allowing the various written works to condemn themselves according to what their revisionist has written.

This book is more than just a Bible comparison study; it will soon become obvious which particular teachings Satan wants to divert us from. The good news is that then the most important truths will be highlighted so that you can now focus on what may have been missing in your life and make it right. We are about to turn over the tables, reversing desolation with revival.

So if in fact the devil has messed with the very Bible translation you have in your hand, is that of concern to you?

At the end of this book you will be required to make a tough decision. You must decide for yourself if you are willing to live with what you discover hidden within the revisions of your favorite Bible translation. Or you must choose to stake your life on the most accurate and at the same time the most maligned Bible translation of all—one that may actually contain the message the Piper doesn't want you to know.

Satan knows he can't destroy the Word of God, but perhaps he can render it ineffectual with the unsuspecting. He knows, better than most of us, which minor deviations he needs to engineer to get us off course from our destiny. His easiest play is to corrupt the written Word so that its readers can bring a curse upon themselves simply by reading or hearing it. Do you believe it is possible for us, though desiring to be faithful Christians by reading our Bible regularly, to actually end up worse off at the end than we were before?

Satan can easily corrupt the Scriptures in a couple of ways. First, he can add to it, but that is risky since those who have studied the Bible for some time would say, "Wait a second! That is not biblical." Or second—the safer route—he can remove or rearrange the content, which is much easier to get away with. Of course the deception is not really obvious; that is why it is so deceptive.

In addition to altering the Word, Satan releases his arsenal of weapons and we don't even realize he has hit the intended target. He knows how to make our Bible reading unproductive in a number of ways. For instance, we may experience a spirit of slumber as soon as we open the Bible to study. Furthermore, a vexation of confusion, misunderstanding, distraction, mind blanking, or mind wandering would frustrate a Bible student who doesn't recognize that the source of the problem may not be with them.

The source of the problem is spiritual in nature, for as soon as you open up the Word of God to escape the kingdom of this world you enter into battle with an unseen enemy who is ruthless and unrelenting with many weapons in his arsenal. Rather than discern the battle zone for what it is, the Bible reader assumes the problem is with the Bible version they are reading, and so they go out and buy whatever is the Bible of the week.

The plethora of Bible renderings available today has created a modern-day fallout reminiscent of the tower of Babel, which saw languages so confused that the people could no longer understand each other. A shepherd teaches from one book and each of the sheep attempts to follow along in a version that doesn't even resemble what they hear. For example, your minister is reading a passage like the following from his New International Version (NIV), which goes like this: "And they went to another village" (Luke 9:56, NIV).

Meanwhile you are following along in another version that is almost four times as long as the minister's translation. "**For the Son of man is not come to destroy men's lives, but to save them.** And they went to another village" (Luke 9:56, AKJV).

We note that not only are the translations different but a very important phrase is missing, a phrase that changes everything. We will take a closer look at what has happened here shortly in this book.

Could you imagine the confusion in a college calculus class where everyone came in with their own textbook and insisted theirs was the best?

Perhaps the easiest of the devil's tactics to recognize is his work to divert us away from a Bible that is accurate and true to the Word of God. Scholarly sorts of vain men are enlisted to ridicule and intimidate anyone who chooses to follow his heart's convictions regarding the preserved Word of God, particularly if he argues for the Authorized King James Version. An easy way to determine which Bible is true would be to listen to a discussion in a seminary classroom on all the translations: the one that is singled out and attracting the most scorn would be the real deal. Sadly, this is not a fabricated statement.

When Satan tried to enlist Balaam to curse the children of Israel he couldn't. So his plot changed to get the men of Israel to curse themselves by tempting them with some beautiful foreign women (Revelation 2:14). It worked better than we could have imagined—in Satan's favor. The nation would soon fall.

Likewise, Satan knows he can't curse the children of God today without a cause. But he has a plan to get us to bring a mountain of the accursed things upon ourselves. We don't even have to preach or read a diminished Scripture text; all we have to do is hear it being taught and give regard to it.

> … every man that **heareth** [give audience or consider] the words of the prophecy of this book, **If any man shall add unto these things,** God shall add unto him the plagues that are written in this book. And **if any man shall take away from**

the words of the book of this prophecy, God shall take away his part out of the book of life, and out of the holy city, and from the things which are written in this Book.

Revelation 22:18-19, AKJV

To those of you that are zealous toward God, may I remind you that we are in the end time. This end time is characterized by a falling away due to apostasy. The meaning of apostasy is divergence from the truth. And when there is a divergence from the truth we have confusion, as these two are like Siamese twins. James 3:16 says that confusion is accompanied by envy, strife, and every evil work.

Let no man deceive you by any means: for that day shall not come, except there come a falling away [defection, apostasy] first, and that man of sin be revealed, the son of perdition....

2 Thessalonians 2:3, AKJV

ONE DEGREE

No one chooses to fall away from the truth. It happens by movements so minute they remain imperceptible. It is like a ship leaving port with the compass set one degree off course. At first no one notices, but five thousand miles later it is realized that the destination was missed by eight hundred miles!

All that God does for us, in us, and through us must be in agreement with His Word. It is the only material the Spirit of God uses to reconcile us unto God and to lead the way to an abundant life. So it should come as no surprise that the archenemy of all mankind would concentrate his efforts to twist the Word of God just enough so that we end our lives off course.

Please be prepared that what you are about to read may be very difficult as the Bible version you have held sacred all your life may in fact be an offense to God. I've had to take the same journey myself, and I know the painful reality of what I'm putting forward. I trust you'll be able to receive this teaching in the gentleness and respect it is intended to convey.

> I will worship toward thy holy temple, and praise thy name for thy lovingkindness and for thy truth: **for thou hast magnified thy word above all thy name.**
>
> Psalm 138:2, AKJV

Would you be willing to let every word you ever uttered define who you are? Our Lord has gone further by saying that He will stand behind every word He proclaimed, even above His own name. Who then has the liberty to trivialize and change His Word?

> For verily I say unto you, Till heaven and earth pass, one jot or one tittle shall in no wise pass from the law, till all be fulfilled.
>
> Matthew 5:18, AKJV

The jot refers to the seemingly most insignificant word or letter, and the tittle is a little accent mark grammarians use. Jesus is simply saying, "Don't mess with the Book!"

You would think then that heaven and earth should have passed away when we look and see that not only jots or tittles but entire phrases and verses have disappeared from many of our most trusted modern variations of the Holy Text.

So why did you go out and buy a modern Bible translation in the first place? Was it because you wanted a Bible that was easier to understand, written in modern and more relevant language? Was it so you could learn God's desire for your life and to develop a closer relationship with Him? Or perhaps you were led to believe that modern scholars had a better handle on the ancient languages? Could it be that people you trusted suggested your particular version was the most accurate to date?

If you found out that your favorite translation—although easier to understand—systematically took away from who Jesus is, actually demoted Him, reduced the consequence of sin, and at the same time elevated Satan, would you still insist on trusting your spiritual life to your modern translation?

One of the most popular translations, the New International Version (NIV), has the following radical changes: 176 titles of deity missing, at least 169 key passages missing from the New Testament (NT) alone, all 31 times that the word "hell" appears in the Old Testament (OT) are eliminated, 9 out of 22 times in the NT the word "hell" is removed, 2922 fewer words, 6653 changes using so-called "dynamic equivalency." The entirety of these verses are missing: Matt. 17:21, 18:11, 23:14; Mark 7:16, 9:44, 9:46, 11:26, 15:28, 16:9-20; Luke 17:36, 23:17; John 5:3-4, 7:53-8:11; Acts 28:29.[1] In 1881 the English Revised Version (ERV) was commissioned by the Church of England to be developed from the Westcott and Hort Text. I know this gets confusing, but the ERV was then "Americanized," and so we have the American Standard Version (ASV), which was revised yet again to the "New" American Standard Bible (NASB). There are at least 5337 deletions noted in the first revision. When you are reading through the NASB you probably wouldn't notice the 35 times the word "Lord" is gone, the 73 times "Jesus" is removed, or the 43 times the word "Christ" is gone,[2] and you might not even notice a phrase in the temptation of Jesus Christ—"Get thee behind me Satan"—is missing completely.

So, if the above statements are true, and vital words have been taken away from the Word of God, would this not be cause for concern?

> And if any man shall take away from the words of the book of this prophecy, God shall take away his part out of the book of life, and out of the

---

1   Floyd Nolen Jones, *Ripped Out of the Bible* (Word of God Publishing, 2004).

2   S. Frank Logsdon, from the recorded sermon "From the NASV to the KJV, Testimony of a Committee Member for the New American Standard Version."

holy city, and from the things which are written in this book.

Revelation 22:19, AKJV

Now, in the event the misbeliever suspected that the omissions might be observed, the revisionists placed a clever note in the margin that says *"Not in the oldest manuscripts!"* or *"Not in the best manuscripts!"* However, they do not tell you which are the oldest or the best. The average man sees such a notation and assumes that these are scholars and therefore must know, and he accepts the alteration. After all, everyone wants to follow the oldest and best manuscripts, right? It is nothing but a clever wording to get us to feel too intimidated to ask questions of our esteemed theologians.

ADVANCES OR DIVERSIONS?

The typical reader may assume the changes have resulted from supposed advances made in the ongoing study of Greek, which have sharpened the reviser's skill in translating.

However, the shocking truth lies in the fact that the modern translations were derived from two radically different Greek revisions. These texts originated from Alexandria, Egypt. One was called the Sinaiticus and the second the Vaticanus. The Sinaiticus was presumably retrieved from a trashcan at St. Catherine's Monastery by German Bible scholar Constantine Tischendorf, and the second was retrieved from a dusty shelf in the Vatican. Though Tischendorf may have retrieved the manuscript, he was aware of over 14,800 alterations and said it is extremely unreliable, containing gross blunders where as many as 40 words are dropped at a time due to a copiest technique.[3] These texts were rejected by the early church in the third to fifth centuries as a depraved Gnostic alteration of the true text, and they were again rejected by Erasmus and the Reformers in the sixteenth century.

Gnosticism is a teaching based on personal mystic revelation knowledge coupled with religious experience that may be traced back to the fifth century BC in Syria and Persia and gaining momentum in Egypt in the second and third centuries AD. *Gnosis* is a Greek word meaning "secret knowledge." Gnostics have rejected the idea of God becoming incarnate in the man Jesus, born of a virgin, who died and rose again bodily to reconcile the lost to their creator, God. One's salvation is essentially a journey of self-consciousness and awareness of one's own divinity through their "secret knowledge." They believe all matter is evil and only the spirit is good, so then God could never present Himself in the flesh of a man. This creates a further problem as they would have to deny Jesus as being part of the Godhead—thus the doctrine of the Trinity would have to be refuted.

---

3   David L. Brown, *Codex Sinaiticus: It Is Old But Is It the Best?* (The Dean Burgon Society, 2013).

The Gnostic doctrine has been popularized by *The Da Vinci Code* and Freemasonry. Obvious influence is also evident in the writings of Scientology, Mormonism, and movements that started out well like the Latter Rain movement and its many tentacles, which opened the door to an unaccountable position due to their "revelation knowledge." Who can question one who prefaces every statement with "God just told me" or "God gave to me special revelation knowledge?" Doctrine tainted with Gnosticism is not limited to a minority group—it is creeping into mainline Christianity through a one-religion worldview.

If I or anyone says "I have a new revelation!" that should trigger your investigator senses to search the Scriptures to see if it is true. The supposed revelation must be found clearly written in the Scriptures.

> Knowing this first, that no prophecy of the scripture is of any private interpretation. For the prophecy came not in old time by the will of man: but holy men of God spake [as they were] moved by the Holy Ghost.
>
> 2 Peter 1:20-21, AKJV

I believe this next passage will be difficult to comprehend. It is not uncommon for God to allow false teachers and doctrines to enter the church as a test to see what we will do with it. Should we stray off course the slightest, it gives testimony to our fickle love of God in favor of an idolatrous teacher.

> If there arise among you a prophet, or a dreamer of dreams, and giveth thee a sign or a wonder, And the sign or the wonder come to pass, whereof he spake unto thee, saying, Let us go after other gods, which thou hast not known, and let us serve them; Thou shalt not hearken unto the words of that prophet, or that dreamer of dreams: for the LORD your God proveth [tests] you, to know whether ye love the LORD your God with all your heart and with all your soul. Ye shall walk after the LORD your God, and fear him, and keep his commandments, and obey his voice, and ye shall serve him, and cleave unto him.
>
> Deuteronomy 13:1-4, AKJV

The apostle John purposed to correct Gnostic heresy, which was prevalent at the time of the early church, in such passages as 1 John 4:1-3 and 1 John 5:6-8.

> Beloved, believe not every spirit, but try the spirits whether they are of God: because many false prophets are gone out into the world. Hereby know ye the Spirit of God: Every spirit that confesseth that Jesus Christ is come in the flesh is of God: And every spirit that confesseth not that Jesus Christ is come in the flesh is not of God: and

this is that [spirit] of antichrist, whereof ye have heard that it should come; and even now already is it in the world.

1 John 4:1-3, AKJV

This scripture addresses the doctrine of Jesus Christ coming in the flesh. Any religion or sect that hints otherwise is of an antichrist spirit and should be shunned. All our religious devotion and sacrifice is in vain if this truth isn't confessed.

The next passage draws another line in stone regarding the oneness of the Godhead consisting of our Father in heaven, His Son Jesus Christ, and the Holy Spirit.

And, furthermore, that there is a very narrow way to the Father and that is through the doorkeeper of life, His son Jesus Christ.

This is he that came by water and blood, even Jesus Christ; not by water only, but by water and blood. And it is the Spirit that beareth witness, because the Spirit is truth. For there are three that bear record in heaven, the Father, the Word, and the Holy Ghost: and these three are one. And there are three that bear witness in earth, the Spirit, and the water, and the blood: and these three agree in one. If we receive the witness of men, the witness of God is greater: for this is the witness of God which he hath testified of his Son. He that believeth on the Son of God hath the witness in himself: he that believeth not God hath made him a liar; because he believeth not the record that God gave of his Son. And this is the record, that God hath given to us eternal life, and this life is in his Son. He that hath the Son hath life; [and] he that hath not the Son of God hath not life.

1 John 5:6-12, AKJV

These words were written so that we may discern false doctrine. Remember these passages as we continue our study to see how these doctrines have been altered to rob men of life.

In the late 1800s two brilliant Catholic scholars, Bishops Westcott and Hort, infiltrated the Church of England posing as teachers and set out to discredit the Authorized King James Version (1611)—and the majority texts from which it was translated into English—by using two doctored texts, the Sinaiticus and Vaticanus.

Out of the 5255 documents of biblical antiquity that exist today, 5210 of those (known as the majority texts) support the AKJV while the remaining 45 documents, or about 1 percent (referred to as the minority texts), support the Sinaiticus or Vaticanus manuscripts that Westcott and Hort used. So when you see the notation "not in the best manuscripts" this is the 1 percent saying that the 99 percent supporting the ancient Scriptures are wrong and truth should be deferred to the recently discovered 1 percenters.

It is from these minority texts that the Westcott and Hort text was derived in Greek and immediately translated into English in the late 1800s as the English Revised Version of the Bible. To promote their new version, Westcott and Hort claimed that their manuscripts were older than all of the 5210 texts used for the AKJV. That statement was simply untrue. The Vatican Scrolls were corrupted with Greek Gnostic philosophy at the Alexandrian School of Gnosticism in Egypt, founded by Philo Judaeus. Westcott and Hort were avid readers of Philo Judaeus, and you'll see the influence of Gnosticism throughout the multitude of Scripture that is omitted or changed in their writings.[4]

You may ask me, "Well, Dennis, does this mean you are King James only?" The question is often asked as if it were a bad thing. No, I am not necessarily a "King James only," but I am "majority text only," and the AKJV is the only surviving easy-to-read English translation of that origin. I insist upon the AKJV as I believe God had His hand in its careful translation. I gladly endure antiquated English knowing that the text is the most accurate to what the Spirit of God wants to say to us. Despite four centuries of fluctuations in the English language, the AKJV is still relevant and unsurpassed in accuracy and understanding.

When you see what has been discovered in these modern translations, you'll understand why there is no way one would even use them as reference in personal Bible

---

4   Samuel C. Gipp, *An Understandable History of the Bible (DayStar, 2004).*

study. *I had to decide if I was a wolf in sheep's clothing or a true shepherd that would stand alone if need be. Oh, there is irony here as I might be of the 1 percent that is troubled by what the Westcott and Hort 1 percenters are up to!*

Doctrines of
Our Departure

In Christianity we have a number of doctrines that define our faith, doctrines of immutable truth. In this section we will explore twenty-four of these defining doctrines to see for ourselves how these truths have been eroded at such a pace that few have noticed the deviation.

As you go through this study of the revisions of biblical text ask yourself the following questions:

1. Is Jesus Christ increased or decreased from His role in the Godhead?
2. Is the change just a difference in interpretation, or does there appear to be a malicious agenda?

3. Do any of the changes advance Satan's kingdom?
4. Is the Word of God lessened or increased?
5. Does the change alter doctrine?
6. Does the change make sense? Does it clarify or confuse?

The final and perhaps most important question would be whether there is evidence to support the claim made earlier regarding Gnostic content in modern Scripture. If substantial evidence is not there, then I have made a slanderous statement. If however the assertion is true, you have a decision to make, and the reason why will soon be evident.

Although the NIV and the NASB are singled out mostly here, they are not alone as all the modern translations, including the Jehovah's Witnesses Bible (New World Translation, or NWT), use the same Westcott and Hort modifications of the minority texts. By comparing the version you may have with the modifications shown here, you will be able to quickly establish which text it originates from and whether you want to be caught dead with it.

1.
Doctrine of the virgin birth

Gnostics deny the deity of Christ and don't believe in the virgin birth. Here you'll see a subtle twist, changing the word "Joseph" in the AKJV to "father" in the NIV. Who was Jesus' Father? It was God! The NASB, Revised Standard Version (RSV), Darby, American Standard Version (ASV), and all the other modern translations that follow Westcott and Hort have the same error.

> And **Joseph** and his mother marveled at those things which were spoken of him.
>
> Luke 2:33, AKJV

By calling Jesus' stepdad by his first name, Joseph, a clear distinction is made as pertaining to the virgin birth.

Can you recognize the subtle shift in the wording of the NIV modification below?

> The **child's father** and mother marvelled at what was said about him.
>
> Luke 2:33 NIV

We know the child's Father was God and His mother Mary. God the real Father would have no need to marvel about what was said of His Son. (See also Luke 2:43.)

2.
Doctrine of the deity of Jesus Christ

Jesus Christ appeared to John to commission him to write the last book of the Bible. To give full authority and blessing to this book, Jesus' deity was proclaimed:

...Saying, I am Alpha and Omega, the first and the last: and, What thou seest, write in a book, and send it unto the seven churches which are in Asia...

Revelation 1:11, AKJV

The modern translations won't give Jesus His proper place and instead show their Gnostic leanings. The vital proclamation highlighted in the above verse is omitted from all the versions that blindly translate from the 1 percent Westcott and Hort texts.

(...?...) which said: "Write on a scroll what you see and send it to the seven churches..."

Revelation 1:11, NIV, NLT, ESV, NASB

A deliberate swipe is made to deny the deity and role of Jesus Christ as He is the Alpha and Omega.

Read the next verse and see if you can discern its origin:

(...?...) saying: "What you see write in a scroll and send it to the seven congregations, in Ephesus and in Smyrna and in Pergamum and in Thyatira and in Sardis and in Philadelphia and in Laodicea."

Any thoughts as to the origin of this verse?

This verse is also Revelation 1:11, but it is from the Jehovah's Witnesses New World Translation (NWT).

As we look at another verse, the Spirit of God wants us to know that life is more than physical, it is spiritual as well—the latter being the most important.

> And Jesus answered him, saying, It is written, That **man shall not live by bread alone, but by every word of God.**
>
> Luke 4:4, AKJV

The NIV will, with the stroke of a pen, eliminate the spiritual, commenting only on the physical.

> Jesus answered, "It is written: 'Man does not live on bread alone.' (...?...)"
>
> Luke 4:4, NIV

The NIV omits the phrase "but by every word of God." Christ is called the "Word," and this is a purposeful omission consistent with the Gnostic teaching of denying the deity of Jesus. This changes the meaning completely. This error is copycatted by the NLT, NASB, RSV, and ASV as evidence, revealing their source as well.

Are you beginning to see that there was more to the revisions than their claim to simply make the texts more readable and easy to understand? In fact we have seen many verses already that don't even make sense because of the way they were altered, and we are just getting started.

For this cause I bow my knees unto the **Father of our Lord Jesus Christ**...

Ephesians 3:14, AKJV

The Holy Spirit desires to remind us constantly of who is the Father of our Lord Jesus Christ, and for good reason. The Spirit of God knew that in latter days there would be a resurgence of false teaching and a denial of the One who changed everything.

For this reason I kneel before the Father (...?...)

Ephesians 3:14, NIV

You may compare the above modifications at a great free online ministry called www.blueletterbible.org if you don't have the two translations handy.

The NLT, NASB, RSV, and ASV follow the same error in deleting the witness of Jesus Christ. With the next verse the change is a little more subtle, but it is still a change. Your turn to be the investigator: what is the difference between the next two verses, and what are the ramifications?

Let this mind be in you, which was also in Christ Jesus: **Who, being in the form of God, thought it not robbery to be equal with God**:

Philippians 2:6, AKJV

Who, being in very nature (?) God, did not consider
equality with God something to be grasped (?)
Philippians 2:6, NIV

The majority text version, the AKJV, unmistakably declares the deity of Jesus Christ: "Who, **being in the <u>form</u> of God, THOUGHT IT NOT ROBBERY TO BE EQUAL WITH GOD.**"

The NIV reads, "Who, being in very **nature** God, DID NOT CONSIDER EQUALITY WITH GOD SOMETHING TO BE GRASPED."

The NIV again subtly perverts the deity of Jesus Christ! The word "form" is replaced with "nature," which puts Jesus Christ on the same level as all men as we are all created in the "image" or nature of God, but we certainly aren't all in the "form" of God.

A careful reading is required to see the subtle switch in wording of the phrase highlighted in captial letters where the NIV translation actually reverses the intended meaning as noted in the AKJV. The AKJV states that Jesus had no hesitation in proclaiming He was equal with God; the NIV says something very different, that Jesus didn't think such a proclamation was necessary or important.

(See also Matt. 18:11, 23:8, 25:13, 28:6; Mark 11:10; Luke 4:4, 9:56; John 4:42, 5:30, 6:39, 6:69, 8:11, 8:29, 16:16; Acts 2:30, 3:26, 4:24, 7:37, 8:37, 15:18; Rom. 1:16, 16:24; Gal. 3:17, 6:15.)

3.

*Doctrine of Satan's ambition
to be as the Most High God*

Let's compare how the AKJV and the NIV esteem Lucifer in Isaiah 14:12.

> How art thou fallen from heaven, **O Lucifer, son of the morning!** how art thou cut down to the ground, which didst weaken the nations!
>
> Isaiah 14:12, AKJV

Now watch what happens to Lucifer:

> O how you have fallen from heaven, **you shining one**, son of the dawn! How you have been cut down to the earth, you who were disabling the nations.
>
> Isaiah 14:12, Jehovah's Witnesses NWT

Where is Lucifer in the New World Translation? Seems he was given an alias to protect him. Let's see if the Jehovah's Witnesses Bible is alone in this.

> How art thou fallen from Heaven, **O morning star, son of the dawn,** you have been cast down to the earth, you who once laid low (?) the nations.
>
> Isaiah 14:12, NIV

In the NIV, Lucifer has been replaced with "O morning star," which is the title for Jesus Christ in Revelation 22:16.

> I, Jesus, have sent mine angel to testify unto you these things in the churches. I am the root and the offspring of David, and the bright and **morning star**.
>
> Revelation 22:16, AKJV

The name Lucifer has completely disappeared from the NIV. Why might that be?

Satan twists the modern translations of the Bible to help fulfill his quest to be as the Most High God noted in his "Five I Wills" of Isaiah 14:13-14.

- I will ascend into heaven
- I will exalt my throne above the stars of God
- I will sit also upon the mount of the congregation
- I will ascend above the heights of the clouds
- I will be like the Most High

Satan usurps worship from Jesus Christ by assuming Christ's title in his modified translations.

Jesus is the Morning Star, and that title is never given to anyone else in the Bible. However, in the versions that use the Westcott/Hort text, we have Jesus Christ and Satan sharing the same title, and the name Lucifer is wiped out: NASB: star of the morning; NRSV: day star; REB: bright morning star; NWT: you shining one; NAB: morning star.

4.

*Doctrine of Satan's desire
to usurp worship from Christ*

Satan not only wants to receive worship himself, he doesn't want Jesus to be worshipped.

> Then came to him the mother of Zebedee's children with her sons, **worshipping him**, and desiring a certain thing of him.
>
> Matthew 20:20, AKJV

> Then the mother of Zebedee's sons came to Jesus with her sons and, **(?)** kneeling down, asked a favor of him.
>
> Matthew 20:20, NIV

> Then the mother of James and John, the sons of Zebedee, came to Jesus with her sons. She **(?)** knelt respectfully to ask a favor.
>
> Matthew 20:20, NLT

Who doesn't want Jesus Christ to be worshipped?

And the devil said unto him, All this power will I give thee, and the glory of them: for that is delivered unto me; and to whomsoever I will

I give it. **If thou therefore wilt worship me, all shall be thine.**

> Luke 4:6-7, AKJV

Satan offers us all that his kingdom has; you can settle for that if that is your only ambition. Not this guy.

It is troubling that we are required by protocol to refer to certain dignitaries today as "Your worship"…really?

(Also see Matt. 8:2, 9:18, 15:25, 18:26, 20:20; Mark 5:6, 15:19.)

5.
Doctrine of the kingdom of God

In Matthew 6:13 the NIV, along with most of the modern modifications, omits the punch line of the Lord's Prayer. Who doesn't want the kingdom of God to be established? Satan. By this omission, millions have failed to pray for the kingdom of God to come. That is very serious.

> And lead us not into temptation, but deliver us from evil: **For thine is the kingdom, and the power, and the glory, for ever. Amen**.
>
> Matthew 6:13, AKJV (word count 25)

> And do not bring us into temptation, but deliver us from the wicked one (…?…)
>
> Matthew 6:13, Jehovah's Witnesses NWT

Does the Jehovah's Witnesses Bible have a friend planted in the evangelical Christian church?

And lead us not into temptation, but deliver us from the evil one. (...?...)

Matthew 6:13 NIV, NLT, ESV, RSV
(word count diminished from 25 to 13)

The NASB has the verse in brackets, which they footnote "probably not in the original writings." If that isn't a red flag! What "original writings" could they be talking about other than the altered Gnostic ones from Alexandria, Egypt? The prayer doesn't even make sense without this concluding phrase. Do you think God would need the word "probably" in His Word?

Let's look at another place where the Lord's Prayer occurs to see what they have done there.

. . .Our Father **which art in heaven**, Hallowed be thy name. Thy kingdom come. **Thy will be done, as in heaven, so in earth.** Give us day by day our daily bread. And forgive us our sins; for we also forgive every one that is indebted to us. And lead us not into temptation; **but deliver us from evil.**

Luke 11:2-4, AKJV (word count 58)

Compare the previous verse with this next one to see what was altered. The NIV removes everything that refers to a holy God in heaven:

Father (...?...), Hallowed be your name, your kingdom come, (...?...) Give us each day our daily bread. Forgive us our sins, for we forgive everyone who sins against us. And lead us not into temptation (...?...)

Luke 11:2-4, NIV

(word count diminished from 58 to 33)

Everything that distinguishes God from the devil is REMOVED! Also it comes as no surprise that the last phrase, "but deliver us from evil," is missing as it asks God to deliver us from Satan's kingdom!

The Spirit of God does not soften words when He speaks of this deceiver and his relationship to the gullible:

Ye are of your father the devil, and the lusts of your father ye will do. He was a murderer from the beginning, and abode not in the truth, because there is no truth in him. When he speaketh a lie, he speaketh of his own: for he is a liar, and the father of it.

John 8:44, AKJV

6.

Doctrine of Jesus Christ coming
to earth to save the lost

For the Son of man is come to save that which
was lost.

Matthew 18:11, AKJV

Unless you were reading ahead of the class you can't
imagine what could possibly need changing in this fantastic
verse. Well, here it is:

[Omitted] Matthew 18:11, NIV
[Omitted] Matthew 18:11, NLT
[Omitted] Matthew 18:11, ESV
[Omitted] Matthew 18:11, NWT

Missing altogether from the Westcott and Hort texts
is the phrase "**For the Son of man is come to save that
which was lost**." Omitting the proclamation denies the
gospel together with the purpose and deity of Christ.
The NLT and RSV omit this, and the NASB, Darby, and
ASV add it in brackets. Just so you know this is no simple
accident, the removal of this same doctrine occurs in Luke:

For the Son of man is not come to destroy
men's lives, but to save them. And they went to
another village.

Luke 9:56, AKJV

What could possibly be the translator's elusive agenda in the following?

(...?...) and they went to another village.
Luke 9:56, NIV, NLT, ASV (diminished from 22
down to 6 words)

At least those who seek to destroy men's lives by altering the Word of God decided it was okay for us to know that "someone went to another village"!

7.
Doctrine of the second coming of Jesus Christ

So intent were the Gnostics to remove the reference to the Son of man that they chopped a scripture so short it no longer made sense: not to mention the fact they caused another error in denying the second coming of Jesus Christ.

Here is the Word as we know it should be:

Watch therefore, for ye know neither the day nor the hour **wherein the Son of man cometh.**
Matthew 25:13, AKJV

But this:

Therefore keep watch, because you do not know the day or the hour (...?...)
Matthew 25:13, NIV

The NIV says, "Therefore keep watch, because you do not know the day or the hour." But it misses "**wherein the Son of man cometh**," which skews the coming of Christ for His church. As you read the NIV it doesn't complete the sentence, so you are left wondering: what are we to keep watch for? If you were to read the entire chapter 25 in the NIV it does not improve. Caught in the same mire again is the NASB, RSV, Darby, and ASV.

In the event you wondered if the NIV is in agreement with the Jehovah's Witnesses Bible:

> Keep on the watch, therefore, because YOU know neither the day nor the hour. (...?...)
> Matthew 25:13, Jehovah's Witnesses NWT

You who have judged, can you still cast the first stone?

8.
Doctrine of repentance

Some of you that have been around for a while, have you ever wondered why there is so little emphasis on repentance in the contemporary church? Could it be that this important process is also eliminated from the modified Bibles the pastors are getting their messages from?

> When Jesus heard it, he saith unto them, They that are whole have no need of the physician, but

they that are sick: I came not to call the righteous,
but sinners to repentance.

> Mark 2:17, AKJV

Isn't the phrase "but sinners to repentance" pivotal to
the message of this passage?

Upon hearing this Jesus said to them: "Those who
are strong do not need a physician, but those who
are ill do. I came to call, not righteous people, but
sinners (…?…)"

> Mark 2:17, Jehovah's Witnesses NWT

On hearing this, Jesus said to them, "It is not the
healthy who need a doctor, but the sick. I have not
come to call the righteous, but sinners (…?…)"

> Mark 2:17, NIV

The same travesty also occurs in Matthew as we
see it here in Mark, so deleting the call to repentance is
no accident.

But go ye and learn what [that] meaneth,
I will have mercy, and not sacrifice: for I am
not come to call the righteous, **but sinners to
repentance**.

> Matthew 9:13, AKJV

Who doesn't want sinners to repent?

Go, then, and learn what this means, "I want mercy, and not sacrifice." For I came to call, not righteous people, but sinners. (...?...)

Matthew 9:13, Jehovah's Witnesses NWT

Now compare to:

But go and learn what this means: "I desire mercy, not sacrifice."* For I have not come to call the righteous, but sinners (...?...).

Matthew 9:13, NIV

In the NIV it states, "I have not come to call the righteous, but sinners." It then omits the last phrase, "**to repentance**." Gnostics do not believe in physical sin, and of course Satan doesn't want people to repent. After all, our refusal to repent keeps him in power. The NLT, NASB, RSV, and Darby follow suit. The result today is that few Christians understand or believe they must repent for their personal sin after making a decision to follow Christ

Jesus singled out the religious leaders as the ones most in need of repentance at the time of His earthly ministry. They were the greatest among the sinners, and yet they thought they were the very finest!

But when he saw many of the Pharisees and Sadducees come to his baptism, he said unto them, O generation of vipers, who hath warned

you to flee from the wrath to come? Bring forth
therefore fruits meet for repentance.

Matthew 3:7-8, AKJV

I think the reason God has called me to be a teacher
is because I had the most to learn. I was among those who
weren't listening very well, thinking I had my Christianity
pretty much in the bag. I would have been included in the
"viper" section.

9.
Doctrine of forgiveness

By now as you read the next verse you will probably be able
to anticipate how a Gnostic scribe might reword it.

But if ye do not forgive, neither will your Father
which is in heaven forgive your trespasses.

Mark 11:26, AKJV

So did you guess that the Gnostic scribe would
eliminate the entire verse?

[No text: the ENTIRE verse is omitted!]

Mark 11:26, NIV, NLT, ESV

Two dashes ("— —") replace the original text in Mark
11:26 of the Jehovah's Witnesses New World Translation.

What a tragedy for a believer who is diligently reading their Bible and yet is totally oblivious to what some men with an agenda did to the text. To miss out on the Spirit's conviction to forgive and let go of the bitterness so that you in turn will be forgiven is as important as breathing. The NLT and RSV omit this verse, and the NASB and ASV have it in brackets, which implies that it is not important.

You can probably already answer the question posed earlier: has anything from the Word of God been diminished?

10.
Doctrine of the Son of God, Jesus Christ, coming in the flesh

Therefore being a prophet, and knowing that God had sworn with an oath to him, that of the fruit of his loins, **according to the flesh, he would raise up Christ to sit on his throne...**

Acts 2:30, AKJV

I believe the NIV's take on this passage may be considered blasphemous:

But he was a prophet and knew that God had promised him on oath that he would place **one of his descendants on his throne.** (...?...)

Acts 2:30, NIV

The NIV agrees with the NWT consistently.

Therefore, because he was a prophet and knew that God had sworn to him with an oath that **he would seat one from the fruitage of his loins upon his throne** (…?…)

Acts 2:30, Jehovah's Witnesses NWT

The prophet referred to here was David, and he was told the Son of God, the Prince of Peace, would be placed on the throne in his lineage. God only has one descendant, and He was named in the original text, yet the NIV has descendants, plural. Is Satan leaving the door open for himself to usurp, according to his ambition? Note that the Mormon translation elevates Lucifer to the spirit brother of Jesus, whereas the original living text leaves no room for such an interpretation for any other messiahs or gods.

In Acts 2:30 the AKJV reads, "**According to the flesh, He would raise up Jesus Christ to sit on His Throne.**" This important phrase, "**According to the flesh,**" is denied in the NIV, NASB, RSV, Darby, ASV, and most others as it attests to Jesus being fully man and fully God.

Is this denial of Jesus that "is come in the flesh" an isolated incident, or is it a repeated deliberate antichrist doctrine of the NIV? Consider Paul's writing in 1 Timothy:

And without controversy great is the mystery of godliness: **God was manifest in the flesh**, justified in the Spirit, seen of angels, preached unto the Gentiles, believed on in the world, received up into glory.

> 1 Timothy 3:16, AKJV

Notice how the King James is very clear in telling us WHO was manifest in the flesh: **GOD was <u>manifest in the flesh</u>**. The flesh is referring to Christ being fully God and fully man. Now watch how the new renderings throw God clear out of the verse: "He appeared in a body" (NIV). He appeared in a body? So what?

Beyond all question, the mystery of godliness is great: He (…?…) appeared in a body, was vindicated by the Spirit, was seen by angels, was preached among the nations, was believed on in the world, was taken up in glory.

> 1 Timothy 3:16, NIV

Everyone has "appeared in a body"! "He" is a pronoun that refers to a noun or antecedent. There is no antecedent in the context of the NIV! The statement does NOT make sense. And folks say the AKJV is difficult to understand! The NIV subtly perverts 1 Timothy 3:16 into utter nonsense.

NASB: He who was revealed in the flesh; NRSV: He was revealed in flesh; LB: Who came to earth as a man; NWT: He was made manifest in the flesh; NAB: He manifested in the flesh.

11.
Doctrine of baptism

You are probably getting tired of the repetition of obliterations in the books we trusted. What would you say if the following verse was missing as well?

> ...what doth hinder me to be baptized? And Philip said, If thou believest with all thine heart, thou mayest. And he answered and said, I believe that Jesus Christ is the Son of God.
>
> Acts 8:36-37, AKJV

> [Oops—they omitted this one as well.]
>
> Acts 8:37, NIV

> [Oops—they too omitted this one.]
>
> Acts 8:37, NLT

> [Oops—what is going on here?]
>
> Acts 8:37, ESV

Why would this verse be eliminated in the NIV, NLT, ESV, NRSV, RSV, Darby, NASB, and NWT? At first glance it would be because of the Gnostic disbelief that Jesus Christ is the Son of God. But there is even more. This verse is very important because it places a definite condition upon water baptism: one must first BELIEVE IN CHRIST!

This would negate the sacrament of infant/child baptism so they changed the Scripture to fit their Roman church dogma. You'll recall that Westcott and Hort were impostors from the Church of Rome planted in the Church of England to discredit the King James Bible and change the Scriptures to match their religious teachings. I realize that some of you may feel offended here, but the Holy Bible trumps all traditions of man, denominations, and state, and the Bible sets the standards for our final judgment.

12.
Doctrine of Jesus Christ's role in creation

Gnostics deny the deity of Jesus Christ, so what does that say about the modern translations if they have the same belief? Of course, if they deny the deity of Christ they would also have to deny reference to Him doing God's works.

> And to make all men see what is the fellowship of the mystery, which from the beginning **of the world** hath been hid in God, **who created all things by Jesus Christ**...
>
> Ephesians 3:9, AKJV

> I was chosen to explain to everyone this mysterious plan that God, the Creator of all things (...?...), had kept secret from the beginning (...?...).
>
> Ephesians 3:9, NIV

What is missing? "**by Jesus Christ**." This would deny Christ's deity, His eternal past as God, and His role in creation. The NLT, NASB, RSV, Darby, and ASV also deny Jesus' role as Creator by leaving out this phrase.

> ...and should make men see how the sacred secret is administered which has from the indefinite past been hidden in God, who created all things. (...?...)
>
> Ephesians 3:9, Jehovah's Witnesses NWT

Who are the false teachers? Do we not know them by their fruit?

13.
Doctrine of the Holy Spirit's role in convicting man of sin

A subtle omission in an important passage in 1 Peter suggests you can purify your soul carnally simply by obedience. The fact is we can't do it on our own, and that is why the Holy Spirit is active in our temple.

> **Seeing ye have purified your souls in obeying the truth <u>through the Spirit</u> unto unfeigned love of the brethren, see that ye love one another with a pure heart fervently...**
>
> 1 Peter 1:22, AKJV

Check out what was checked out:

> Since you have **in** obedience to the truth (...?...) purified your souls for a sincere love of the brethren, fervently love one another from the heart...
>
> 1 Peter 1:22, NASB

The love spoken of here in the majority text (AKJV) is *agape*, which is a gift of the Holy Spirit that is empowered by the Spirit. It is the love spoken of in the Great Commandment. In my book *Sanctiprize* we look at how important this is to understand. The modern translations make it impossible to be obedient to the one commandment we are to get right.

> Now that you have purified yourselves by obeying the truth (...?...) so that you have sincere love for your brothers, love one another deeply, from the heart.
>
> 1 Peter 1:22, NIV

The NIV, NLT, NASB, RSV, Darby, and ASV omit "**through the Spirit**" after the phrase "...obeying the truth." This omits the Holy Spirit's role in convicting us of our sin.

The first part of this next verse is often quoted but without the necessary caveat: there is a condition for living without condemnation.

> There is therefore now no condemnation to them
> which are in Christ Jesus, **who walk not after the
> flesh, but after the Spirit.**
>
> Romans 8:1, AKJV

The altered versions have left off the caveat, which
would imply condemnation or judgment for sin; there is
condemnation for those who walk after the flesh.

> Therefore, there is now no condemnation for
> those who are in Christ Jesus (...?...)
>
> Romans 8:1, NIV, NLT, NASB

Is the author of this revision at all concerned with
the believer finishing well so that sin doesn't become his
damnation?

Several men brought to Jesus a woman caught in
adultery. The point of the story is that the accusers were
guilty of the same sin they accused the woman of:

> And they which heard it, **being convicted by
> their own conscience,** went out one by one,
> beginning at the eldest, even unto the last: and
> Jesus was left alone, and the woman standing
> in the midst. When Jesus had lifted up himself,
> and saw none but the woman, he said unto her,
> **Woman, where are those thine accusers?** Hath
> no man condemned thee?
>
> John 8:9-10, AKJV (word count 63)

Sadly, what is missing in the Bibles of most churches is the role of the Spirit's conviction through our conscience and the identification of the accuser.

> At this, those who heard (...?...) began to go away one at a time, the older ones first, until only Jesus was left, with the woman still standing there. Jesus straightened up and asked her, "Woman (...?...) where are they? Has no one condemned you?"
>
> John 8:9-10, NIV, NLT, ESV, RSV, NASB
> (word count diminished from 63 to 43)

Do you perceive that it is a dangerous thing to read a book that grievously tramples upon the role of the Holy Spirit?

14.
Doctrine of cleansing our temple

There is a silver lining in going through this comparison of scriptures. Every omission has a purpose to divert you from God and His Son and to keep you in rebellion to the Word of God. So understand that the omissions are key diversions by Satan so he can keep his kingdom in power. Reverse the omissions and you will be an overcomer. Now you know what things are the most important for you to get right!

> For ye are bought with a price: therefore glorify
> God in your body, **and in your spirit, which
> are God's**.
>
> 1 Corinthians 6:2, AKJV

It is our spirit that requires cleansing so the Holy Spirit can reside within. Satan doesn't want you to glorify God in your spirit as that would leave him without a home.

> …you were bought at a price. Therefore honor
> God with your body (…?…).
>
> 1 Corinthians 6:2, NIV, NLT, ESV, NASB

The most vital part of our relationship with God is accomplished through our spirit. Without the work of the Holy Spirit in our lives it is impossible, absolutely impossible, to honor God with our body.

15.
Doctrine of the Trinity or Godhead

The same books that have been written to expose the lies in the Jehovah's Witnesses Bible (NWT) should very well include all the modern Bible translations used by the majority of churches. Many mainline denominations and non-denominational churches alike have made the NIV their official Bible. Even worse, some have made a so-called living paraphrase their choice. Some of the highest selling

Christian books on the market jump from version to version with no concept as to what the Spirit must say to us.

In this section the question needs to be asked: which version here carefully preserves the doctrine of the Trinity and is easiest to understand, even for a child?

> For there are three that bear record in heaven, the Father, the Word, and the Holy Ghost: and these three are one.
>
> 1 John 5:7, AKJV

> So we have these three witnesses (...?...)
>
> 1 John 5:7, NLT

> For there are three that testify (...?...)
>
> 1 John 5:7, NIV

> For there are three that testify (...?...)
>
> 1 John 5:7, NASB

> For there are three witness bearers (...?...)
>
> 1 John 5:7, Jehovah's Witnesses NWT

All the NIV has here is "For there are three that testify (...?...)." Missing is the Godhead: "**in heaven, the Father, the Word, and the Holy Ghost: and these three are one.**" They wouldn't be trying to deny the Godhead or the Trinity would they? The Godhead is also missing in the NASB, RSV, NLT, ESV, VUL, Darby, ASV, and others.

Don't use any version other than the AKJV when witnessing to Jehovah's Witnesses. They'll point you to your NIV to refute the Godhead, knowing that your NIV (and the other modern translations) agrees with their altered Bible, the New World Translation. The NWT is also contrived from the Westcott and Hort texts as they share many of the same Gnostic beliefs. Sorry to say, but if you have been using most any of the modern translations and have pointed out to a Jehovah's Witness that their Bible is altered, you are guilty of having the same possession.

16.
Doctrine of the Judgment Seat of Christ

But why dost thou judge thy brother? or why dost thou set at nought thy brother? For we shall all stand before the **judgment seat of Christ.**

Romans 14:10, AKJV

Can you guess from the previous verse what might have been removed from a Bible that adheres to Gnosticism?

You, then, why do you judge your brother? Or why do you look down on your brother? For we will all stand before God's judgment seat.

Romans 14:10, NIV

The NIV, NASB, RSV, Darby, NLT, ESV, and ASV fail again to magnify Jesus Christ as the Father intended.

They all replace the "**judgment seat of Christ**" with the "judgment seat of God." Again, this is done to deny the power and purpose of our personal Lord and Savior.

17.
Doctrine of scientific understanding

The Bible is very scientific and holds many truths that science has yet to catch up with. I will address a few hundred of these scientific certainties in a new book series coming soon titled *Yada Bits*.

> O Timothy, keep that which is committed to thy trust, avoiding profane and vain babblings, and oppositions **of science falsely so called**…
>
> 1 Timothy 6:20, AKJV

Many lies are being propagated today in the name of "science" (evolution for example), but 1 Timothy 6:20 has been warning us about it all along—except in the new versions where "science" is translated as the following: NIV: knowledge; NASB: knowledge; NRSV: knowledge; LB: knowledge; NWT: knowledge; NKJV: knowledge.

> Timothy, guard what has been entrusted to your care. Turn away from godless chatter and the opposing ideas of what is **falsely called knowledge**…
>
> 1 Timothy 6:20, NIV

"Concerning Darwin," Hort said, "it is a treat to read such a book. My theory is strong that the theory is unanswerable. If so it opens up a whole new period." (Note that Hort's English, although two hundred years later than when the AKJV was written, is most difficult to understand.) Is it okay for a translator of the Bible to be from the enemy's camp?

The science in the Bible is intended to help the scientific mind recognize the existence of God. The biblical science is astonishing; if you have been studying the Bible with the modern works you will have missed out on most of these astonishing finds.

18.
Doctrine of redemption

...in whom we have redemption **through his blood,** even the forgiveness of sins.

Colossians 1:14, AKJV

Satan hates the atoning blood of the Lord Jesus Christ, so we shouldn't be surprised to find the reference "**through his blood**" missing in the versions in which he orchestrated a rewrite:

...in whom we have redemption (...?...), the forgiveness of sins.

Colossians 1:14, NIV

...who purchased our freedom (...?...) and forgave our sins.

> Colossians 1:14, NLT

To understand what the big deal is, we need to understand that Satan's destruction is by the blood of the Lamb.

> And I heard a loud voice saying in heaven, Now is come salvation, and strength, and the kingdom of our God, and the power of his Christ: for the accuser of our brethren is cast down, which accused them before our God day and night. And **they overcame him by the blood of the Lamb**, and by the word of their testimony; and they loved not their lives unto the death.
>
> Revelation 12:10-11, AKJV

What kingdom would dismiss the absolute necessity of noting that our redemption is "through the blood of Christ"? The enemy's deception here makes my blood boil! (Also see 1 John 5:13.)

19.
Doctrine of the believer's warfare

God has taught us how to defeat Satan and how to be delivered from his vexation. Jesus told His disciples that the reason they couldn't defeat the spirit of the lunatic was because they needed to fast.

> Howbeit this kind goeth not out but by prayer and fasting.
>
> Matthew 17:21, AKJV

Would Satan be interested in us knowing how to have him removed?

> [No text for this verse]
>
> Matthew 17:21, NIV

> [No text for this verse]
>
> Matthew 17:21, NLT

> [No text for this verse]
>
> Matthew 17:21, ESV

The shepherds of our flocks have been taught from these altered texts in their seminaries and learned their Greek and Hebrew from the Westcott and Hort Gnostic versions. Hence they are clueless regarding the cleansing of the devil's works—so very few people that should be healed are healed. The book *Sanctiprize* brings this knowledge back to the body of Christ. Such understanding is not possible through any other English translation than the authorized King James

Bible because of its strong adherence to the inspired majority texts.

20.
Doctrine of Satan

When Peter blew it, Jesus wanted to teach him that the words that came out of his mouth were not his but Satan's so Peter would learn discernment of his own spirit.

> And Jesus answered and said unto him, **Get thee behind me, Satan:** for it is written, Thou shalt worship the Lord thy God, and him only shalt thou serve.
>
> Luke 4:8, AKJV

Again, what kingdom would want to remain unrecognized for its stuff? The very one that had the name Lucifer removed from the modern reworks of Scripture. The rebuke of Satan is removed.

> Jesus answered (...?...) "It is written: 'Worship the Lord your God and serve him only.'"
>
> Luke 4:8, NIV

So if your pastor was teaching on the temptations of Jesus Christ from the NIV, you would miss out on the best weapon you have available to defeat a similar satanic attack on yourself.

We can know what just happened was no accident as we see the same pattern repeated in Luke 9.

> But he turned, and rebuked them, and said, Ye know not what manner of spirit ye are of.
>   Luke 9:55, AKJV

When the disciples wanted to call down fire to destroy some folks, the Lord pointed out that they were speaking on behalf of an unclean spirit. So likewise, if you determine your spirituality from the NIV, then Satan will remain at work doing what he does best—and that is to destroy.

> But Jesus turned and rebuked them (...?...)
>   Luke 9:55, NIV

Which kingdom are these diversions in favor of? Is that okay with you? If you are a shepherd of the sheep, of what spirit are you?

21.
Doctrine of healing

Christ equipped the disciples and the church to be able to heal the sick through the purging of the disease's unclean spirit.

> And he ordained twelve, that they should be with him, and that he might send them forth to preach,

And to have power to heal sicknesses, and to cast out devils…

Mark 3:14-15, AKJV

The new versions leave out the reason one might want to be delivered from an evil spirit. Many denominations have trouble with this, and that is why their leaders subscribe to Bibles that agree with their self-adjusting doctrine.

And He appointed twelve, so that they would be with Him and that He could send them out to preach, (…?…) and to have authority to cast out the demons.

Mark 3:15, NASB, NIV, ESV, NLT

Please fill in the blank.

Jesus says He was assigned by God to complete five very necessary works for the church.

The Spirit of the Lord is upon me, (1) because he hath anointed me to preach the gospel to the poor; (2) **he hath sent me to heal the brokenhearted, (3) to preach deliverance to the captives,** (4) and recovering of sight to the blind, (5) **to set at liberty them that are bruised**…

Luke 4:18, AKJV

Out of five purposes for which Christ was sent we have two, arguably three, that remain in the novel versions: (1) and (4).

> "The Spirit of the Lord is on me, (1) because he has anointed me to preach good news to the poor (...?...) He has sent me to proclaim freedom (...?...) for the prisoners and (4) recovery of sight for the blind, to release the oppressed...
> Luke 4:18, NIV, NASB, NLT, ESV

I believe it is our choice of Scripture that is preventing revival by removing the power, favor, and thus anointing of the Spirit of God. (Also see Luke 8:43.)

22.
Doctrine of fasting

One of the greatest moves of God in this age was brought about by the fasting of a devout man, Cornelius. Fasting ushered in the Gentile church.

> And Cornelius said, Four days ago **I was fasting** until this hour; and at the ninth hour I prayed in my house, and, behold, a man stood before me in bright clothing...
> Acts 10:30, AKJV

Due to the significance of this event, you would expect the practice of fasting to shout from the pages of the new generation of Bibles. How disappointed I was to find out the intentional silence.

> Cornelius answered: "Four days ago (...?...) I was in my house praying at this hour, at three in the afternoon. Suddenly a man in shining clothes stood before me."
>
> Acts 10:30, NIV, NASB, NLT, ESV, RSV

Jesus teaches that fasting is sometimes necessary to set free a person that is bound by psychological infirmity.

> Howbeit this kind goeth not out but by prayer and fasting.
>
> Matthew 17:21, AKJV

If you are trusting the Lord for healing and deliverance there is a group of Bibles you need not bother to open:

> [Omitted]
>
> Matthew 17:21, NIV, NASB, NLT, ESV

Gone from the church doctrine is not only fasting but also the healing that results from spiritual purging. Paul taught that the practice of fasting is to be used in our family as well:

Defraud ye not one the other, except it be with consent for a time, that ye may give yourselves **to fasting** and prayer; and come together again, that Satan tempt you not for your incontinency.

1 Corinthians 7:5, AKJV

Pharisees and Westcott and Hort do not agree with Paul or Jesus regarding fasting, and they just removed it from at least three key teaching scriptures on the practice.

Do not deprive each other except by mutual consent and for a time, so that you may devote yourselves to prayer (…?…). Then come together again so that Satan will not tempt you because of your lack of self-control.

1 Corinthians 7:5, NIV, ESV, NLT, NASB

23.
Doctrine of hell

Have you ever wondered why few pastors preach about hell today? Hell is an uncomfortable word, and everybody knows what it means, and they don't want to go there.

The new Bible versions remove the word "hell" wherever possible and replace it with Sheol, Gehenna, Hades, Tartarus, the place of the dead, death, among the dead, the pit, depth, or the grave.

Correct me if I am wrong, but wasn't the intent of the modern versions to make Bible reading and understanding of the truth easier? Let's look at some of the stunts the translators pulled to hide the word hell. Hades is the phonetic version of the Greek word for hell in the NT; Sheol is the phonetic version of the Hebrew word for hell in the OT; *Tartaroo* is an ancient Greek term for hell from which Tartarus is derived; the phonetic version of *geena* (of Jewish origin) resembles Gehenna. Why not just call hell for what it is…HELL?

In Isaiah 14:15 the King James Bible condemns Lucifer to hell: "Yet thou shalt be brought down to hell . . . ." The NIV does *not* condemn Lucifer to hell! The NIV reads, "But you are brought down to the **grave**. . . ." Why doesn't the NIV want Satan in hell? The NKJV takes him down to Sheol; the NLT takes him down to the lowest depths and others to the pit.

Hell is only used by the NIV in the NT when a phrase like "hell fire" occurs, and they just can't use "grave fire" as it would be too obvious of an alteration.

In the OT the AKJV has separate terms like tomb or sepulchre when describing where a person's body is placed upon their death, whereas the word hell is reserved as the place of torment for those who so choose. The NIV calls them all the grave. This completely muddies the meaning, which is their intent. Getting rid of the "thees and thous" was just an excuse and a diversion to cover up the more sinister plot of the translators. It's like bandits staging a car accident near a bank to divert attention from the real crime, which is the holdup inside the bank.

The psalmist says that the wicked and the nations that ignore God will go to hell. What do the modern revisions imply? Or obscure?

> **The wicked shall be turned into hell,** and all the nations that forget God.
>
> Psalm 9:17, AKJV

I think the message above is loud and clear. But can we say that of the following?

> The wicked **will return to Sheol** [Hebrew word for *hell*], even all the nations who forget God.
>
> Psalm 9:17, NASB, ESV, RSV

> The wicked **return to the grave** (...?...), all the nations that forget God.
>
> Psalm 9:17, NIV

Many false teachers across the entire religious spectrum don't believe in hell, or life after death for that matter, so the NIV aids and abets their cause by saying the wicked just die in the grave. What a surprise they'll be in for when they realize the temperature!

In this next Proverb the warning is against the man that seeks out the adulteress. The destination for that type of lifestyle is very evident in the AKJV.

Her house is **the way to hell**, going down to the chambers of death.

Proverbs 7:27, AKJV

Which kingdom would want to soften the blow for those given to fornication and adultery?

Her house is the way to **Sheol**, descending to the chambers of death.

Proverbs 7:27, NASB, ESV, RSV

Sheol sounds like the name of a brothel or something. Not exactly anything to cause a young man to turn in his tracks.

Her house is a highway to the **grave**, leading down to the chambers of death.

Proverbs 7:27, NIV, NLT

The purpose of discipline is so that our sons will not suffer in hell.

Thou shalt beat him with the rod, and **shalt deliver his soul from hell**.

Proverbs 23:14, AKJV

Wow, look at the misleading of the NLT! By getting disciplined physically one will not die—they've discovered the fountain of youth!

Physical discipline may well **save them from death**. (...?...)

> Proverbs 23:14, NLT

You shall strike him with the rod and **rescue his soul from Sheol**.

> Proverbs 23:14, NASB, RSV

By choosing to follow the ways of this temporal world, of which Satan is god, by default we make a covenant with hell. That destiny can be altered now, thanks be to God, as we read in the AKJV.

And your covenant with death shall be disannulled, and <u>**your agreement with hell shall not stand**</u>; when the overflowing scourge shall pass through, then ye shall be trodden down by it.

> Isaiah 28:18, AKJV

Compare with:

Your covenant with death will be canceled, and your pact with **Sheol** (...?...) will not stand; when the overwhelming scourge passes through, then you become its trampling place.

> Isaiah 28:18, NASB, ESV, RSV

To dodge the grave is simply not even close to what is required to cancel our contract with hell.

I will cancel the bargain you made to cheat death,
and I will overturn your deal to dodge the **grave**
(...?...). When the terrible enemy sweeps through,
you will be trampled into the ground.

Isaiah 28:18, NLT

In the NT the modern translators have the same
problem with telling the truth about hell.

Because thou wilt **not leave my soul in hell**,
neither wilt thou suffer thine Holy One to see
corruption.

Acts 2:27, AKJV

For thou wilt not abandon my soul to **Hades**, nor
let thy Holy One see corruption.

Acts 2:27, ESV, NASB, RSV, ASV, YLT, DBY

For you will not leave my soul among **the dead** or
allow your Holy One to rot in the **grave**.

Acts 2:27, NIV

The AKJV has only one word for hell and that is
"hell," and it occurs fifty-four times in the Bible. Though
distasteful, it is so simple that a child can understand what
the Spirit is saying.

We discovered in our study that it wasn't just the actual
word hell that Westcott and Hort wanted to erase but also
other references that related to eternal punishment. This is

also evidence of Gnosticism, or whatever you might want to call it. It is false teaching designed to deceive and alter our destiny.

> Where their worm dieth not, and the fire is not quenched.
>
> Mark 9:44, AKJV

> [Oops—this verse was not invited!]
>
> Mark 9:44, NIV

Not only is the actual word hell removed, but so is its effect, as the deceitful teachers will have us to be ignorant of this eventuality.

> That whosoever believeth in him **should not perish**, but have eternal life.
>
> John 3:15, AKJV

> That everyone who believes in him (...?...) may have eternal life.
>
> John 3:15, NIV

The NIV omits the phrase "**should not perish**," which is a reference to hell. This is the verse before the most-quoted John 3:16. The NLT, NASB, RSV, and ASV also didn't think it was important to remind us about hell here.

Even in more remote references to judgment for sin, the apostate authors of the NIV cleaned out the evidence.

For which things' sake the wrath of God cometh
on the children of disobedience...

> Colossians 3:6, AKJV

Who will receive the wrath of God?

Because of these, the wrath of God is coming
(...?...).

> Colossians 3:6, NIV

Once again, who will receive the wrath of God, and
what does it consist of?

> **In flaming fire taking vengeance** on them that
> know not God, and that obey not the gospel of
> our Lord Jesus Christ...

> 2 Thessalonians 1:8, AKJV

In the distorted version, the removal of the reference
to hell is just too obvious:

> (...?...) He will punish those who do not
> know God and do not obey the gospel of our
> Lord Jesus.

> 2 Thessalonians 1:8, NIV

You may want to do your own comparison study to see
if what I am saying is true: Deut. 32:22, 2 Sam. 22:6; Job
11:8, 26:6; Ps. 16:10, 18:5, 55:15, 86:13, 116:3, 139:8;

Prov. 5:5, 9:18, 15:11, 15:24, 27:20; Isa. 5:14,14:9 and 15, 28:15 & 18, 57:9; Ezek. 31:16 and 17, 32:21 and 27; Amos 9:2; Acts 2:27 and 31; and Matt. 16:18.

24.
Doctrine of truth

The devil is called the father of lies in the AKJV Bible, and I'm sure he doesn't like that title. Of all the commands he could omit, he erases the command not to bear false witness—to lie!

> For this, Thou shalt not commit adultery, Thou shalt not kill, Thou shalt not steal, **Thou shalt not bear false witness**, Thou shalt not covet; and if there be any other commandment, it is briefly comprehended in this saying, namely, Thou shalt love thy neighbour as thyself.
>
> Romans 13:9, AKJV

> The commandments, "Do not commit adultery," "Do not murder," "Do not steal," (…?…) "Do not covet,"* and whatever other commandment there may be, are summed up in this one rule: "Love your neighbor as yourself."
>
> Romans 13:9, NIV

Satan, the father of lies, does not want the church to implicate him in the failure of the church.

O foolish Galatians, who hath bewitched you, **that ye should not obey the truth**, before whose eyes Jesus Christ hath been evidently set forth, crucified among you?

Galatians 3:1, AKJV

By striking the phrase "**that ye should not obey the truth**" from the record, the meaning of the verse is changed and Satan remains completely unchallenged yet again.

You foolish Galatians, who has bewitched you (...?...), before whose eyes Jesus Christ was publicly portrayed as crucified?

Galatians 3:1, NASB, NIV

WHAT DOES THE WORD
SAY ABOUT THE WORD?

There is righteous judgment for changing, reading, or hearing such alterations of the most sacred of writings. This judgment is proclaimed in advance for us in the next verses. These verses are authentic.

By the end of this book you will have to make a decision. Before you continue on though, here are some passages that deal with the offense of adding, diminishing, or messing with the Word of God:

. . . ye have PERVERTED the words of the living
God. . . .

Jeremiah 23:36, AKJV

Ye shall not add unto the word which I command
you, **neither shall ye diminish ought from it**, that
ye may keep the commandments of the LORD
your God which I command you.

Deuteronomy 4:2, AKJV

For verily I say unto you, Till heaven and earth
pass, one jot or one tittle shall in no wise pass from
the law, till all be fulfilled.

Matthew 5:18, AKJV

Heaven and earth shall pass away: but my words
shall not pass away.

Luke 21:33, AKJV

For I testify unto every man that heareth the words
of the prophecy of this book, If any man shall add
unto these things, God shall add unto him the
plagues that are written in this book: And if any
man shall take away from the words of the book of
this prophecy, God shall take away his part out of
the book of life, and out of the holy city, and from
the things which are written in this book.

Revelation 22:18-19, AKJV

Who does God hold accountable for the sin of adding or taking away from His Words in the Bible? Obviously those that would teach, preach, and write from an altered Bible, but now the hearer is also singled out. It is a very serious thing to know this and to ignore it. My heart was so grieved when I saw this for the first time and even more now as I write this. The reason is because we have brought the plagues of the Revelation upon us through a carefully orchestrated scheme of the devil. The church not only gave him an open door but also promoted him, starting in our religious schools to get our professors, then our pastors, and finally most of our authors.

Note: Used properly this list can be an excellent guide of what the devil doesn't want you to know! The doctrines that would weaken or expose the works of Satan, the god of this world, are modified to keep him in power and the Christian powerless.

For further study:

- *Ripped Out of the Bible* by Floyd Nolen Jones
- *Which Version Is the Bible?* by Floyd Nolen Jones
- *King James, His Bible, and Its Translators* by Lawrence M. Vance
- www.blb.org (a highly recommended place to study the Bible safely)

THE NIV AND ZONDERVAN

A little known fact: in 1988, Harper & Row Publishers (now HarperCollins Publishers) purchased Zondervan Publishers and the NIV translation.

HarperCollins is a subsidiary of the global media empire The News Corporation, owned by Rupert Murdock. The News Corporation includes Fox Broadcasting, Twentieth Century Fox, and more than 128 newspapers. Fox Broadcasting produces some of the most lewd shows on television. Murdock also publishes the British newspaper

The Sun, notorious for its nude pinups and unlawful privacy invasion.

Every time you purchase the NIV and many other top-selling modern Bibles, you are giving money to people who produce writings that would make even the residents of Sodom and Gomorrah blush! What about the Satanic Bible? Yes, HarperCollins, under the imprint of Avon, prints the Satanic Bible by Anton La Vey.

Can two walk together, except they be AGREED?
Amos 3:3, AKJV

Jesus Christ plainly said in Matthew 7:17-18: "Even so every GOOD tree bringeth forth GOOD fruit; but a CORRUPT tree bringeth forth EVIL FRUIT. A good tree cannot bring forth evil fruit, neither can a CORRUPT tree bring forth GOOD FRUIT."

Do you really believe God would allow His Holy Word to be "owned" and copyrighted by that group? Is truth and righteousness a priority for the Murdock group?

For what fellowship hath RIGHTEOUSNESS with UNRIGHTEOUSNESS? And what communion hath light with darkness?"
2 Corinthians 6:14, AKJV

THE MEN BEHIND THE
WESTCOTT AND HORT TEXT

Brooke Foss Westcott (1825-1901) and Fenton John Anthony Hort (1828-1892) were the two "scholars" who produced the Greek text of the modern versions. Their dominating influence on the revision committee of 1871-1881 accounts for most of the corruption that we have today in modern translations. The Bible believer should keep several points in mind when discussing these two men. The following information is well documented in: *Final Authority*, by William Grady; Riplinger's *New Age Bible Versions*; *The Life and Letters of Brooke Foss Westcott*, by his son, Arthur Westcott; and *The*

Life and Letters of Fenton John Anthony Hort, written by his son, Arthur Hort.

1. Together, *The Life and Letters of Brooke Foss Westcott* and *The Life and Letters of Fenton John Anthony Hort* run over 1800 pages. A personal salvation testimony is not given once for either man, and the name "Jesus" is found only nine times!

2. Westcott was a firm believer in Mary worship, and Hort claimed that Mary worship had a lot in common with Jesus worship. This is consistent with the allegation that they were Roman Catholic masqueraders in the Church of England.

3. Hort believed in keeping Roman Catholic sacraments.

4. Hort believed in baptismal regeneration as taught in the Catholic Church.

5. Hort rejected the infallibility of Scripture and contended that God never intended the Bible to teach doctrines. He approached the Scriptures as any other prose: Shakespeare, Plato, or Dickens.

6. Hort took great interest in the works of Charles Darwin, while both he and Westcott rejected the literal account of creation.

7. Westcott did not believe in the second coming of Christ, the Millennium, or a literal heaven. He said the destruction of Jerusalem in AD 70 was the second coming spoken of in the Bible.

8. Both men rejected the doctrine of a literal hell, and they supported prayers for the dead in purgatory.

9. Hort refused to believe in the Trinity or the Godhead.

10. Hort denied the existence of angels.

11. Westcott confessed that he was a communist by nature.

12. Hort confessed that he hated democracy in all its forms. While working on their Greek text (1851-1871), and while working on the Revision Committee for the Revised Version (1871-1881), Westcott and Hort were also keeping company with "seducing spirits and doctrines of devils" (1 Tim. 4:1). Both men took great interest in occult practices and clubs. They started the Hermes Club in 1845 (Hermes is the son of Zeus of Greek mythology, noted as the founder of astrology, alchemy, and magic); the philosophical position of Hermetica is that matter is evil and to be escaped—a belief that parallels with Gnosticism. They founded the Ghostly Guild in 1851 (they are acknowledged as the fathers of modern channeling). Hort joined a secret club called The Apostles in the same year. They also started the Eranus Club in 1872. These were spiritualist groups that believed in such unscriptural practices as communicating with the dead (necromancy).

13. The Westcott and Hort Greek text was *secretly* given to the Revision Committee without public

debate or debate from learned scholars of other theological camps.

14. The members of the Revision Committee of 1881 were sworn to a pledge of secrecy in regard to the new Greek text being used, and they met in silence for ten years.

15. The corrupt Greek text of Westcott and Hort was not released to the public until just five days before the debut of the Revised Version Bible. This prevented Bible-believing scholars like Dean Burgon from reviewing it and exposing it for the piece of trash that it was.

16. Hort said, "I am inclined to think that such a state as Eden (I mean the popular notion) never existed."

17. In support of his real identity as a Catholic plant in the Church of England, Hort said, "The Romish view seems to be nearer, and more likely to lead to the truth than the Evangelical…We dare not forsake the sacraments or God will forsake us."

18. Westcott proclaimed, "It is very small, with one kneeling-place; and behind the screen was a 'pieta' [Mary and a dead Christ]…Had I been alone I could have knelt there for hours."

19. We don't have to wonder about Westcott's view of creation either: "No one now, I suppose, holds that the first three chapters of Genesis, for example, gives a literal history."

20. In the Bible, the first mention of Alexandria, where the manuscripts used by Westcott and Hort were found, is in Acts 6:9. Men from that city brought false accusations against Stephen and had him stoned to death. This is the city where the school of Gnosticism was located and where the texts were altered.

A well-orchestrated cyber attack can exploit a weakness to render the largest defense systems in the world useless; a well-orchestrated (demonic) principality attack can exploit a weakness to render the greatest institution, the church, as virtually ineffectual.

The following excerpt is from an article by Dr. Frank Logsdon, "Why We Use the King James Version" (publication date unknown).

Drs. Hort and Westcott together collated the New Testament text. The "new" Greek text was in contrast with and in distinction to the text material that had been received by virtually all Bible believing churches for the preceding 19 centuries; the Majority Text. From the minority text and its direct predecessor, the Westcott and Hort Text, virtually all modern translations and versions of the Bible have been translated into English.

WE BELIEVE THAT THE CRITICAL MINORITY TEXT IS CORRUPT! Not only are its origins and associations suspect, the actual text itself is full of deletions and dilutions of the time honored Scripture. Modern translations based upon the critical text have diluted reference to the blood of Jesus Christ, the Deity of Christ, the inspiration of the Scriptures and salvation by faith to mention a few. There are thousands of textual changes.

If a survey benchmark has been moved or altered, all surveying after that point will be distorted. And because the critical text is in our view corrupt, any version of the Bible translated from it is suspect.

Trouble with the NASB—
and a Most
Heartbreaking Apology

D r. Frank Logsdon was the cofounder of the
New American Standard Bible (NASB). He
since has renounced any connection to it, and
this is his confession:

> I must under God renounce every attachment
> to the New American Standard Version. I'm
> afraid I'm in trouble with the Lord . . . We laid
> the groundwork; I wrote the format; I helped
> interview some of the translators; I sat with the
> translator; I wrote the preface . . . I'm in trouble;

I can't refute these arguments; it's wrong, terribly wrong . . . The deletions are absolutely frightening . . . there are so many . . . . Are we so naive that we do not suspect Satanic deception in all of this?

Upon investigation, I wrote my dear friend, Mr. Lockman, (editor's note: Mr. Lockman was the benefactor through which the NASB was published) explaining that I was forced to renounce all attachment to the NASV (same as the NASB).

You can say that the Authorized Version (AKJV) is absolutely correct. How correct? 100% correct . . . .

Dr. Frank Logsdon
"From the NASV to the KJV"

The publishers of the NASB attempt to distance themselves from Logsdon, even going as far as to claim that he had nothing to do with its creation. Odd that if this were true Mr. Logsdon devoted the better part of the later years of his life to travel and repent so as to warn people about what he had done.

THE KING JAMES VERSION
AND ITS TRANSLATORS

Unlike Westcott, Hort, and the Revised Version Committee, King James went through great efforts to guard the 1611 translation from errors and to be fully accountable and transparent.

1. In 1604, King James announced that fifty-four Hebrew and Greek scholars of the highest esteem had been appointed to translate a new Bible for English-speaking people. The number was reduced to forty-seven by the time the work formally began in 1607.

2. Rather than working together all at one location, these men were divided into six separate groups, which worked at three separate locations. There were two at Westminster, two at Oxford, and two at Cambridge.

3. Each group was given a selected portion of Scripture to translate.

4. Each scholar made his own translation of a book and then passed it on to be reviewed by each member of his group.

5. The whole group then went over the book together.

6. Once a group had completed a book of the Bible, they sent it to be reviewed by the other five groups.

7. All objectionable and questionable translating was marked and noted, and then it was returned to the original group for consideration. The KJV translators were extremely careful regarding any word changes, which were mainly due to idiom changes, and highlighted them in italics.

8. A special committee was formed by selecting one leader from each group to work out all of the remaining differences and present a finished copy for the printers in 1611.

9. This means that the King James Bible had to pass at least *fourteen* examinations before going to press.

10. Throughout this entire process, any learned individuals of the land could be called upon

for their judgment, and the churches were kept informed of the progress.

11. Part of the religious establishment of that day was desperate to keep the King James Bible out of the hands of the English common people. A Jesuit priest, Henry Garret, and Guy Fawkes conspired to have twenty kegs of explosives placed in the basement of the parliament buildings in England to stop King James from completing his work. They were caught and hanged.

12. The majority texts used by King James translators can be traced to Antioch, Syria, which is where Paul and Barnabas taught for a whole year and where believers were first called "Christians" (Acts 11:26). It was a hub of activity for the early church.

13. **The AKJV is a literal word-for-word translation**. When the translators had to add words for sentence structure they placed them in italics or in brackets. The **NIV uses a translation method called "dynamic equivalence."** Rather than a word-for-word translation, the translators added, changed, and subtracted to make the verse say what they "thought" it should. The preface to the NIV even says ". . . they have striven for more than a word-for-word translation. . . ."

Now here's a most interesting thing. The psalmist proclaims that "The Words of the LORD are purified seven times." The fact is that the King James Version is the seventh English Bible to be written. It was translated with a committee of scholars that remains unsurpassed to this day. They had translation tools and understanding that have since been lost, probably because such ability would no longer be required for such translation work, as one might determine from Psalm 12:7.

> Verse 6: The words of the LORD are pure words: as silver tried in a furnace of earth, purified seven times.

> Verse 7: Thou shalt keep them, O LORD, thou shalt preserve them from this generation for ever.

> Verse 8: The wicked walk on every side, when the vilest men are exalted.
>
> Psalm 12:6-8, AKJV

I've had a burning question in my heart for years: why are all the modern translations derived from the minority texts while the AKJV is the last one originated from the majority text? For me that question was answered when I read Psalm 12 and understood its significance. You see, the Word of God was purified seven times, and that version would be preserved alone from that generation back in 1611 until the end of the age.

The first six English translations in order were: Tyndale's, Matthew's, Coverdale's, the Great Bible, the

Geneva Bible, and the Bishops' Bible. The King James is the seventh.[5]

If this understanding is more than just coincidence, and I believe it is, then Psalm 12:8 may refer to the men who have exalted themselves in the translations from then until this day. How many men have dared to name a version of the Bible after themselves! Westcott and Hort are almost worshipped in theological circles for their perceived scholarship.

In this study we haven't even looked at an extremely popular Bible written by Eugene Petersen, *The Message*. In a recent interview he stated bold-facedly that he did not hold to the inerrancy of Scripture and said it is but a story of God's relationship with mankind (author's paraphrase).

In his confessional testimony, *The Testimony of S. Franklin Logsdon,* Dr. Frank Logsdon said, "We've had the AKJV for almost 400 years. It's been tested as no other piece of literature has ever been tested. Word by word; syllable by syllable. And think even until this moment no one has ever found any wrong doctrine in it, and that's the main thing. He that wills to do the will of God shall KNOW the doctrine."

---

5   Laurence M. Vance, *King James His Bible and Its Translators* (Vance Publications, 2006), 84.

THE NEW KING JAMES VERSION

We will now give some special attention to one of the most deceptive translations on the market, the New King James Version, first published in 1979. It is a deceptive version because its editors have succeeded in deceiving the body of Christ on two main points: (1) that it's a King James Bible (which is a lie), and (2) that it's based on the Textus Receptus, or the majority text (which is only a partial truth).

There's nothing "new" about the NKJV logo, the triquetra. Some believe it is a "666" symbol of the pagan trinity that was used in the ancient Egyptian mysteries.

It was also used by Satanist Aleister Crowley around the turn of the twentieth century and by the Wiccan as it symbolizes the triple-aspected goddess (maid, mother, and crone). The symbol can be seen on the New King James Bible, on certain rock albums (like Led Zeppelin's), or you can see it on the cover of such New Age books as *The Aquarian Conspiracy*. (See Riplinger's tract on the NKJV.)

1. It is estimated that the NKJV makes over one hundred thousand translation changes, which comes to **more than eighty changes per page and about three changes per verse**! A great number of these changes bring the NKJV in line with the NIV and the RSV. Where changes are not made in the text, subtle footnotes often give credence to the Westcott and Hort Greek Text.

2. While passing itself off as being true to the majority text, the NKJV ignores the majority text over twelve hundred times.

3. In the NKJV, there are twenty-two omissions of "hell," twenty-three omissions of "blood," forty-four omissions of "repent," fifty omissions of "heaven," fifty-one omissions of "God," and sixty-six omissions of "Lord." The terms "devils," "damnation," "JEHOVAH," and "new testament" are completely omitted.

4. The NKJV demotes the Lord Jesus Christ. In John 1:3, the AKJV says that all things were made "by"

Jesus Christ, but in the NKJV, all things were just made "through" Him. The word "Servant" replaces "Son" in Acts 3:13 and 3:26. "Servant" replaces "child" in Acts 4:27 and 4:30. The word "Jesus" is omitted from Mark 2:15, Hebrews 4:8, and Acts 7:45.

5. The AKJV tells us, in Titus 3:10, to reject a "heretick" after the second admonition. The NKJV tells us to reject a "divisive man." How convenient! Now the Alexandrians and ecumenicals have justification for rejecting anyone they wish to label as "divisive men." A heretic is an adherent to false doctrine. However, with the clever word change of the NKJV, a person can be declared divisive for disagreeing with the heretic!

6. As a final note, I'd like to point out how the NKJV is very inconsistent in its attempt to update the language of the AKJV. The preface to the NKJV states that previous "revisions" of the AKJV have "sought to keep abreast of changes in English speech," and also that they too are taking a "further step toward this objective." However, when taking a closer look at the language of the NKJV, we find that oftentimes they are stepping *backwards*! Please note a few examples of how well the NKJV has "kept abreast of the changes in the English language":

SCRIPTURE	AKJV	NKJV
Ezra 31:4	little rivers	rivulets
Psalm 43:1	judge	vindicate
Psalm 139:43	thoughts	anxieties
Isaiah 28:1	fat	verdant
Amos 5:21	smell	savor
Matthew 26:7	box	flask
Luke 8:31	the deep	the abyss
John 10:41	did	performed
Luke 19:11-27	pounds	minas
John 19:9	judgment hall	Praetorium
Acts 1:8	bowels	entrails
Acts 18:12	deputy	proconsul
Acts 21:38	uproar	insurrection
Acts 27:30	boat	skiff
Hebrews 12:8	bastard	illegitimate

READABILITY TESTS AND ARCHAIC WORDS

According to a Flesch-Kincaid Grade Level research study, the King James Bible is by far the easiest. Out of 26 different categories, the authorized King James graded easier in a whopping 23. In selected analyses, the AKJV average grade level was 5.8—the NIV was 8.4![6]

The Holy Spirit anticipated that future believers would be faced with archaic words, and a pattern was set out on how to handle it.

---

6   Riplinger, *New Age Bible Versions* (A.V. Publications, 1993), 195-209.

Note in 1 Samuel 9:9 below what is in parentheses "(…)", which means the original author of the book wanted to provide commentary on the inspired Word of God. By the way, the brackets "[…]" indicate insertions the AKJV committee made with the text to make it more readable in English. The writer noted the archaic word "seer" was coming up in the text and that it now means "a prophet." However, in verse 11 the word "seer" is not replaced with the more modern word "prophet" as the writer would not tamper with the Word. So in keeping with this teaching, we will simply provide commentary on the more difficult parts of the Word to aid in our understanding.

> (Beforetime in Israel, when a man went to enquire of God, thus he spake, Come, and let us go to the seer: **for [he that is] now [called] a <u>Prophet</u> was beforetime called a <u>Seer</u>.**) Then said Saul to his servant, Well said; come, let us go. So they went unto the city where the man of God [was]. [And] as they went up the hill to the city, they found young maidens going out to draw water, and said unto them, Is the **seer** here?
>
> 1 Samuel 9:9-11, AKJV

We can see how dangerous it is to trust any modern-day publisher to rewrite God's Word accurately. God is totally capable of preserving His Word, and as He inspired the original writings, He will inspire us to understand it accurately.

THOSE THEES AND THOUS

A "pronoun" is a word that "stands in for" another noun or noun-phrase. A "personal pronoun" is one which stands for a person. The personal pronouns are classified as first person, second person, and third person by their relationship to the one speaking. The speaker himself and any others he chooses to include as part of his "group" is called first person. The person(s) TO WHOM the speaker is speaking is called second person. The person(s) ABOUT WHOM the speaker is speaking is called third person. Thus we have the following table which we can construct in English once we differentiate between the purposes of the various pronouns:

	Nominative	Objective	Possessive
1st singular	I	Me	My (or mine)
1st plural	We	Us	Our (or ours)
2nd singular	Thou	Thee	Thy (or thine)
2nd plural	Ye	You	Your (or yours)
3rd singular	He/She/It	Him/Her/It	His/Hers/Its
3rd plural	They	Them	Their (or theirs)

Let's look at a scripture to appreciate why those "thees and thous" actually may be necessary for proper interpretation of a text:

> And **thou** shalt speak unto him, and put words in his mouth: and I will be with **thy** mouth, and with his mouth, and will teach **you** what **ye** shall do.
>
> Exodus 4:15, AKJV

These words of God, spoken to Moses regarding Aaron, are among numerous examples in Scripture where the King James translation uses several different forms of the second-person pronoun. In this one verse, we see the words "thou," "thy," "you," and "ye," all fulfilling this function.

Most modern translations would translate this sentence: "You shall speak to him . . . and I will be with your mouth ... and will teach you what you shall do." Why would the King James translators use four different forms of the pronoun when only "you" and "your" are used in modem versions?

The fact is that Elizabethan-age English was able to make much finer distinctions than modem English. That is, "thou," "thee," "thy," and "thine" were used for the second person singular, whereas "ye," "you," "your," and "yours" were the corresponding words for the plural. Different words also were used for subject, object, and possessive modifier, as is still true for first- and third-person pronouns.

In our text, God was telling Moses that he (Moses) was to speak to Aaron, and that He (God) would then teach both of them, not just Moses, what they were to do. This distinction is clear in the King James English, but not in modern English. This is one of numerous examples where such fine points in the King James language are lost in modern translations.

> You shall speak to him and put words in his mouth;
> I will help both of you speak and will teach you
> what to do.
>
> Exodus 4:15 NIV

In the Lord's Prayer, for example, "Yours is the kingdom" could suggest that many will possess the kingdom, whereas "thine is the kingdom" clearly recognizes one God alone. Clear words are important for clear meanings.

You will notice that replacing "thou/thee/thy/thine" with the ambiguous "you" does NOT clarify, but tends to muddy the Scriptures.

The words of the LORD are pure words: as silver tried in a furnace of earth, purified seven times. Thou shalt keep *[guard, protect, retain]* them, O LORD, thou shalt preserve *[guard with fidelity]* them from this generation for ever.

Psalm 12:6-7, AKJV (emphasis author's)

If one has difficulty in understanding the Authorized King James Version of the Bible, there would be a scrambler, a confusing or slumbering vexation at work in their mind. For further understanding on that refer to the book *Sanctiprize*.

BABEL REBUILT

I believe that as God confounded the language at Babel, Satan, the Piper, has his own thing going in the church. He confounds the Word of God in the pews as the sheep try in vain to follow along in their modern versions, while the shepherd reads from another—and it may be that God meant to convey something different altogether.

For God is not the author of confusion *[disorder, instability]* but of peace, as in all churches of the saints.
  1 Corinthians 14:33, AKJV (emphasis author's)

If God is not the author of confusion then who is?

Therefore shall the strength of Pharaoh be your shame, and **the trust in the shadow of Egypt your confusion.**

Isaiah 30:3, AKJV

The modern translations that rely on the Westcott and Hort version of omissions originate from the altered Gnostic scrolls from Alexandria, Egypt—thus the source of the shadow of confusion cast over our churches.

Has anything changed since the methods Satan used in the garden?

Now the serpent ... said unto the woman, Yea, hath God said, Ye shall not eat of every tree of the garden? And the woman said unto the serpent, We may eat of the fruit of the trees of the garden: But of the fruit of the tree which is in the midst of the garden, God hath said, Ye shall not eat of it, neither shall ye touch it, lest ye die. And the serpent said unto the woman, Ye shall not surely die... For God doth know that in the day ye eat thereof, then your eyes shall be opened, and ye shall be as gods, knowing good and evil. And when the woman saw that the tree was good for food, and that it was pleasant to the eyes, and a tree to be desired to make one wise, she took of the fruit thereof, and did eat,

and gave also unto her husband with her; and
he did eat.

Genesis 3:1-6, AKJV

Now the Piper says, "The Scriptures are too hard to
understand, and you are missing out on all that God has
to teach you. How could you be cursed for reading a Bible
that is easier to understand? That is not what God meant!"

Pastors that were professionally trained in the original
languages most likely studied exclusively from the Westcott
and Hort version of Greek and Hebrew as opposed to the
majority texts as cited at the beginning of this writing.

Whosoever therefore shall be ashamed of me
and of my words in this adulterous and sinful
generation; of him also shall the Son of man be
ashamed, when he cometh in the glory of his
Father with the holy angels.

Mark 8:38, AKJV

My conviction, in order to be able to understand
Jesus "as the scripture hath said" (John 7:38), is to use
the Authorized King James Version exclusively with study
aids such as Strong's Concordance to help understand the
original languages.

Every major revival in the last three hundred years has
been based on the AKJV. Since all these new translations
have hit the churches we have not had any major revivals
except revivals initiated by the likes of Chuck Smith—a

staunch advocate of the AKJV—of the Jesus Movement in the 1970s. According to historians, there were "awakenings" around the years 1727, 1792, 1830, 1857, 1882, and 1904. More recent revivals include those of 1906 (Azusa Street), 1930s (Balokole), 1970s (Smith, Jesus People), and 1909 (Chile Revival). All these incredible awakenings occurred before the AKJV was supplanted.

Copy Right or Wrong?

The NIV came out in 1978 and the NASB in 1971. Depending on which list you use these translations are at least the 65th in the succession of English translations written. The popular *The Message* is about the 148th. My understanding is that for a book to get a copyright it has to be at least 60 percent different from any and every version that preceded it. I'm no mathematician, but as I calculated it, in order for the tenth consecutive book to get a copyright it would end up having only 1 percent in common with the first book printed.

No one would go through the expense of rewriting the Bible unless they could copyright the material as being their own—and that is the point — the material is their own. The Authorized King James Version is not copyrighted, and it is not known if it ever was. The only thing that can be copyrighted in a AKJV Bible is maps and study notes inserted by the respective publisher.

Regardless of what I or any mortal may say, the Spirit of God anticipated that the written Word would be secretly tampered with and exacts the penalty.

> But there were false prophets also among the people, even as there shall be false teachers among you, who privacy *[secretly alter biblical truth]* shall bring in damnable *[resulting in loss of eternal life]* heresies *[carnal doctrine],* even denying the Lord that bought them, and bring upon themselves swift destruction. And many shall follow their pernicious *[leading to destruction and misery]* ways; by reason of whom the way of truth shall be evil spoken of. And through covetousness shall they with feigned words make merchandise of you: whose judgment now of a long time lingereth not, and their damnation slumbereth not.
>
> 2 Peter 2:1-3, AKJV (emphases author's)

Some questions to consider from this discerning passage:

Q. Are the changes in the new versions crafty, secret, or hidden from view?

Q. Are one or more groups interested in perverting the gospel to authenticate their doctrines (Gnostics, denominations, *The Watch Tower*, Scientology, Satan, evolutionists, New Agers, atheists, or proponents of the emergent church, spiritual formations, or contemplative prayer, etc.)?

Q. If you follow these false teachers' pernicious ways through their Bibles, what is a possible consequence if you do not repent?

Q. Is the way of truth evil spoken of? Absolutely. If you say you will only use the AKJV they'll call you narrow (that's actually good), old-fashioned, "King James Only People," fundamental …

I have no problems with the definition of fundamental from Oxford's dictionary: "A form of Protestant Christianity which upholds belief in the strict and literal interpretation of the Bible, including its narratives, doctrines, prophecies, and moral laws. They oppose social and political liberalism and reject the theory of evolution."

You'll be told how smart the scholars are; you'll be told that King James was gay (that was a fabrication made by a fellow dismissed from the translation team), and you'll be informed of the higher text criticism that is now available, and who are you to judge them? Still ringing in my ears is the angry retort I got from a pastor friend who informed me of my lowly status and his own proficiency in the biblical language and the fact that he was a Greek professor in a seminary. Take your peace as I have because you know who is behind these accusations.

It is now necessary to reconsider the questions asked at the beginning of this section:

- Is Jesus Christ increased or decreased?
- Is the change just a difference in interpretation, or is there a malicious agenda?
- Do any of the changes boost Satan's kingdom?
- Is the Word of God diminished or expanded?
- Does the change alter doctrine?
- Does the change make sense? Does it clarify or confuse?

One final word from the Word for sheep and shepherd:

Take heed therefore unto yourselves, and to all the flock, over the which the Holy Ghost hath made you overseers, to feed the church of God, which he hath purchased with his own blood. For I know this, that **after my departing shall grievous wolves enter in among you, not sparing the flock. Also of your own selves shall men arise, speaking perverse things, to draw away disciples after them**...And now, brethren, I commend you to God, and to the word of his grace, which is able to build you up, and to give you an inheritance among all them which are sanctified.

Acts 20:28-32, AKJV

Now comes your part: you must make a decision to accept what you have discovered herein, repent, turn and seek forgiveness regarding your participation with the work of an antichrist spirit—or determine the problems raised here are trivial and no action is required on your part. But you must make a decision for you and your house. King Belshazzar was shown by deed and word how to honor the LORD, but when it mattered most in his life, when unbeknown to him he was being tested, he was weighed in the balances and found wanting.

You may consider how things have been working in your spiritual life and ministry thus far, and ask the Lord to show you what He sees. Ask Him to show you the mystery of godliness (1 Timothy 3:16).

There is a blessing for those who are courageous, especially in the face of change and opposition. I hope you have chosen in such a manner that this blessing is yours.

> Be strong and of a good courage: for unto this people shalt thou divide for an inheritance the land, which I sware unto their fathers to give them. Only be thou strong and very courageous, that thou mayest observe to do according to all the law, which Moses my servant commanded thee: turn not from it to the right hand or to the left, that thou mayest prosper whithersoever thou goest.
>
> Joshua 1:4-6, AKJV

In times of old, God looked around to find a man willing to make up the hedge and stand in the gap before Him so He would not have to destroy the nation, but He found none. I believe God is still looking to see who will take the fidelity test and be found faithful to His Word, thus declaring their single-minded love and devotion to Him.

If revival were to depend on you as a King's messenger... will revival happen?

If we may we be of further service to you, please visit us at www.mystrongtower.com.

Our Ministry: My Strong Tower Ministries
'a place for learning, restoration & celebration'
www.mystrongtower.ca

Our Home: www.1000IslandsVillage.com
Our Address: My Strong Tower Ministries
             1120 County Road 2 E,
             Brockville, Ontario, Canada
             K6V 5T1

Dennis Bank is devoted to see individuals get the one thing that they must get right in life right! Dennis, his wife Margaret and family are the founders of My Strong Tower Ministries located in the 1000 Islands Village near Brockville, Ontario. Dennis has developed life-altering seminars including "Marriage Isn't for Cowards" and "My Strong Tower Summit" as well as the Victory Lap Bible School and the thought provoking Yada` Bits scientific series.

You'll want to read the other books by Dennis Bank:

Sanctiprize: *Restoration to the Person you were created to be, Holy & Without Blame, Embodying the Father's Love.* **www.sanctiprize.com**

Yada` Bits, the series ...coming soon. **www.truthco.co**

Printed in the USA
CPSIA information can be obtained
at www.ICGtesting.com
JSHW080001150824
68134JS00021B/2213

9 781614 488064